D1611925

MONSTERS

HYDRA

BY JENNIFER GUESS McKERLEY

KIDHAVEN PRESS
A part of Gale, Cengage Learning

GALE
CENGAGE Learning™

Detroit • New York • San Francisco • New Haven, Conn • Waterville, Maine • London

GALE
CENGAGE Learning™

LIBRARY OF CONGRESS CATALOGING-IN-PUBLICATION DATA

McKerley, Jennifer Guess.
  Hydra / by Jennifer Guess McKerley.
    p. cm. — (Monsters)
  Includes bibliographical references and index.
  ISBN 978-0-7377-4081-3 (hardcover)
  1. Hydra (Greek mythology)—Juvenile literature. I. Title.
  BL820.H93M35 2009
  398'.469—dc22

                                           2008029074

KidHaven Press
27500 Drake Rd.
Farmington Hills, MI 48331

ISBN-13: 978-0-7377-4081-3
ISBN-10: 0-7377-4081-7

Printed in the United States of America
2 3 4 5 6 7 12 11 10 09

Printed by Bang Printing, Brainerd, MN, 2nd Ptg., 11/2009

CONTENTS

CHAPTER 1

GREAT MULTI-HEADED MONSTER

The Hydra was called the destroyer of men. She was a huge water beast with nine snake heads. The name *hydra* comes from an old Greek word for water. The imaginary serpent first appeared in Greek tales and songs that date back to the eighth and seventh centuries B.C. According to an ancient book of myths, one of the monster's nine heads was immortal. It would live forever. The head was even said to be made of gold. Some people who retold the story gave the Hydra fewer than nine heads, and some gave it a hundred heads or more. No matter how many heads the beast had, the Hydra caused terror wherever she went. It was only natural that the Hydra behaved

The Hydra of legend is a monstrous multi-headed serpent found in Greek tales and songs dating back nearly 3,000 years.

Great Multi-Headed Monster

5

horribly. She came from monster parents made only for battle.

Legend tells us that Mother Earth created the Hydra's parents to fight the god Zeus. He ruled Mount Olympus, the highest mountain in Greece. Zeus reigned over lesser gods called the Olympians, but he wanted to command the entire universe. This meant he had to overthrow the older gods, Mother Earth's first children—the Titans.

Fight for the Universe

Zeus hurled his thunderbolts at the Titans. Even Atlas, the strongest of their warriors, could not stand against him and his lightning weapons. The Titans lost, and Zeus reigned over the universe. Now Mother Earth bellowed with fury. Zeus had locked the Titans in a deep, sunless place called **Hades.** He also sent Atlas to the edge of the world and placed the heavy Earth on his shoulders. In her anger, Mother Earth created two hideous monsters, Typhon and his mate, Echidna. Then she sent them to attack Zeus and the Olympians.

Hydra

The enormous Echidna, half woman and half snake, ate men raw. Her husband, Typhon, had 100 serpent heads that reached to the stars. Poison and

Zeus hurls a thunderbolt in his victorious battle against the Titans for command of the universe.

flames shot from his wicked eyes. His dark flickering tongues spewed lava and fiery stones and made a terrifying hissing sound. A hundred more snakes sprouted from his thighs. Typhon and Echidna appeared so frightening that when the two approached, the Olympian gods shape-shifted into the forms of animals and escaped. Typhon ripped up whole mountains and flung them at the fleeing Zeus.

Yet Zeus turned around, his courage restored. When the other gods saw him, they rushed back to help, and a dreadful battle began. The sky and the seas churned with rage. Lands near and far shook. Great storm waves and hot winds covered the Earth and killed almost every living thing. As Typhon aimed another mountain at the gods, Zeus fired off a hundred thunderbolts. They struck the mountain and pushed it back down on top of Typhon. According to legend, he stayed there forever to spew lava and fumes through the top of Mt. Etna, a volcano in Sicily. Zeus defeated Typhon, but now he had to deal with Echidna.

BIRTH OF THE SHE-MONSTER

Typhon's ghastly wife retreated to give birth to their monster children. She hid in a cave, where she ate all who passed by outside. Echidna tried to charm Zeus. She made the woman part of herself appear lovely with beautiful eyes and flawless skin. Zeus spared Echidna's life but not because of her

beauty. Instead, he decided to let her and her grue-some children live so they could serve as a test for brave heroes to come.

Echidna gave birth to the Hydra. The baby's writhing snake heads spewed breath so poisonous

A sculpture depicts Hydra's mother, Echidna, a half-woman, half-snake monster created by Mother Earth to defeat Zeus and the other Olympian gods.

that the fumes overcame most creatures who ventured close. A single drop of her blood also proved deadly. If one of her nine heads got cut off, two new heads instantly grew in its place.

Echidna also gave birth to beastly brothers and sisters for the Hydra and became known as the Mother of All Monsters. A brother, the ferocious Nemean lion, had skin so tough no weapon could pierce it. The Chimera exhaled scorching fire. She had a front like a lion, a middle like a goat, and a back end like a snake. Another sister, the Sphinx, was a winged lion with a woman's head. She told a riddle to all who came her way and ripped them in two when they failed to solve it. Two brothers, Cerberus and Orthus, were dogs with snakes for tails. Cerberus had three heads, and Orthus had two. Zeus's wife, Queen Hera, took the baby Hydra and raised it so she could later use the monster against her enemies. She nurtured the serpent in the wetlands of Lake Lerna.

DEEP AND DANGEROUS

Although the Hydra is a make-believe monster, Lake Lerna, where the serpent made her home, is a real place. The lake dried up long ago. Still, modern **geologists** believe they have located the site of the ancient freshwater lake. The site is in southern Greece, south of the city Árgos. (Árgos is thought to be the oldest city in the country.) Diggings by geologists have uncovered evidence that

people lived in Lerna as far back as 5000–4900 B.C. According to legend, Lake Lerna was one passage to the underworld. Old writings show that people long ago believed the waters of Lake Lerna had healing powers—that is, if humans dared to step in. People in the city also thought the Alcyonian Lake, connected to Lake Lerna, was bottomless and treacherous. Humans took a deadly risk when they entered the waters. In his book, *Guide to Greece*, Pausanias, a Greek author in the second century A.D., wrote about these beliefs.

> There is no limit to the depth of the Alcyonian Lake, and I know of nobody who by any contrivance [means] has been able to reach the bottom of it since not even Nero [an emperor of Rome], who had ropes made several stades long and fastened them together, tying lead to them, and omitting nothing that might help his experiment, was able to discover any limit to her depth. This, too, I heard. The water of the lake is, to all appearance, calm and quiet but, although she is such to look at, every swimmer who ventures to cross her is dragged down, sucked into the depths, and swept away.[1]

The Hydra made the lake and nearby countryside her domain, and she became known as the Lernaean Hydra. She attacked humans, raided

Marshes remain in the region of Greece where Lake Lerna, the legendary home of the Hydra and a portal to the Underworld, was once found.

flocks, and ruined the land. Although the Hydra roamed and terrorized, the war between the gods came to an end.

BIRTH OF HYDRA'S ENEMY

Mother Earth gave up her grudge against Zeus, and the lands and seas recovered from the damages of war. Now Zeus wanted many human wives and Earthly children. Such offspring would be half di-

Hydra

vine and half human, so Zeus thought they would become great heroes and heroines for Greece. Often he disguised himself as a human man and sneaked down to Earth in search of pretty women—like Princess Alcmene.

In time, Hercules was born to Zeus and Alcmene. A jealous Queen Hera tormented Alcmene and her son. While Hercules was still in the cradle, Hera sent two spotted snakes to attack him. Hercules merely gripped a serpent in each baby hand and crushed them to death. When he grew up, Alcmene sent Hercules into the mountains near Thebes to protect the sheep herds from roaming predators. Soon he had killed all the lions and wolves in the area. His fame spread, and Hercules became known as the strongest man ever to walk the Earth.

The king of Thebes admired Hercules so much he gave his daughter to him in marriage. Then Hera caused Hercules to become insane. In a crazed state, he thought his family was a group of wild beasts. He killed them all. When Hera allowed his mind to return to normal, Hercules became

A Roman sarcophagus depicts Hercules engaged in the twelve labors assigned to him by King Eurystheus after he murdered his family in a fit of madness.

grief-stricken. He sought the advice of the **oracle of Delphi**. He had to know what he must do to make up for his horrible deeds. The oracle told Hercules to serve his cousin Eurystheus as a slave for a decade. He would also have to complete ten labors as ordered by Eurystheus.

Although Eurystheus was a king, he was weak. He also despised his strong, famous cousin. Hera knew she could influence the king to give Hercules the worst possible tasks. For the first four labors,

Hydra

Eurystheus directed Hercules to kill all the threatening beasts and monsters in the countryside. The first monster Hercules sought was the Nemean lion, which he squeezed to death with his bare hands. His next task would be to travel to Lake Lerna to slay the ferocious multi-headed serpent.

CHAPTER 2

HYDRA REARS HER UGLY HEADS

Hercules' nephew, Iolaos, drove him in a chariot to Lake Lerna, where Hercules spied the Hydra on a stone ledge. Her tail twitched as Hercules shot flaming arrows. The monster raised her enormous serpent body and turned toward him. Nine long necks thrashed. Nine snake heads hissed. Eighteen pairs of evil eyes narrowed as fangs prepared to strike. Hercules caught hold of one of the necks and struck the head with his club. The Hydra wrapped her long necks around his feet and attempted to knock him down. Again he swung his club. One of the hissing snake heads tumbled to the ground. Then to his shock, two snake heads instantly grew back in place of the

16

one. More black tongues flicked. More sharp fangs lunged at Hercules. His club swung through the air and knocked off the two new heads. The necks squirmed and spurted blood. Within a second, four new heads sprang up.

Hercules used all his strength to fight back. The deadly fumes and blood of the Hydra would have

Hercules battles the Hydra, knocking off her snake heads while Iolaos uses a torch to sear the stumps to keep additional heads from sprouting.

killed any other human, but Hercules, half god and half man, did not succumb. Yet he could not defeat the Hydra. Every time he cut off a head, it was replaced by two more. Then Athena, goddess of wisdom, sent word from the heavens that he must use fire to defeat the great serpent.

SLAYING OF THE HYDRA

Hercules called Iolaos and instructed him to set fire to some trees and use the burning branches as torches. Now they worked together. As soon as Hercules knocked off one of the Hydra's heads, Iolaos held fire to the wriggling stump. The flames scorched the budding heads on the stumps of the necks and prevented their growth.

The vengeful Hera realized Hercules might defeat her precious serpent. She sent a giant crab to pinch his foot with its huge claws. Hercules flung his leg out in pain and launched the crab into the air. It landed, crushed on the ground. Hercules turned back and knocked off more heads while Iolaos quickly singed the necks. Soon there remained only the ninth head—the immortal one, the gold one. Hercules lopped it off. He held the severed snake head in his hands. Still alive, it hissed and raised its fangs. Hercules knew he could not kill it so he dug a deep hole and buried the head. Then he placed a heavy boulder over the grave. As Hercules chopped up the gigantic serpent body, he pulled out one huge tooth to save. Then he dipped

his arrows in the Hydra's **venom**. Now he had arrows laced with a potent poison. Whatever he hit with his arrows would die. In the heavens, Hera roared. She picked up the dead crab and placed it in the skies to become a constellation, or group of stars.

Although the eternal head stayed alive, it was trapped underground. The Hydra could cause no more harm. At least, that is what Hercules thought. He traveled on to finish the rest of his labors, which included battles with more of the Hydra's siblings. Directed by Hera, Eurystheus declared that Hercules' defeat of the Hydra did not count because his nephew had helped him. He added extra tasks for Hercules to perform. In the end, Hercules completed twelve labors.

Hydra Strikes Back

Later Hercules married Deianira, another lovely princess. One day at a rushing stream, Hercules tested the waters and forded the stream safely. Before he could go back to carry Deianira across, the **centaur** Nessus passed by. Like all centaurs, Nessus was fond of lovely maidens and decided to kidnap Deianira. He galloped off with the screaming bride. Hercules fired one of his arrows that had been dipped in the Hydra's venom. It hit Nessus in the back, and he collapsed. Yet before Nessus died, he vowed to himself to get revenge against Hercules. He pulled off his shirt. It was soaked with his

 Hydra

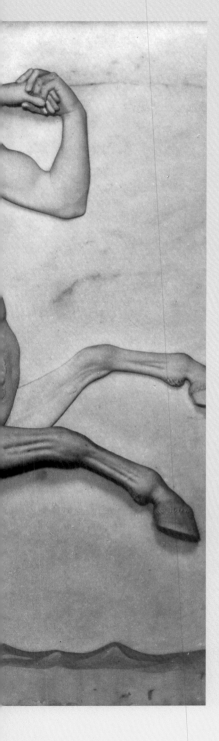

blood that was now mixed with the serpent's venom. He handed the shirt to Deianira and told her to save drops of blood from it for a good luck charm. He said if she ever thought her husband loved another, she must paint the blood on Hercules' tunic. Then Hercules would love only her. Deianira squeezed out drops of blood and stored them. She feared Hercules would someday desire other wives.

Soon after Hercules won an impressive victory and wanted his best tunic to wear for the celebration. He sent a messenger home to tell his wife. Yet she believed Hercules desired to dress up to impress a woman. She smeared the drops of blood she had saved on Hercules' coat. Then she sent it off.

The centaur Nessus kidnaps Hercules wife, Deianira, only to be killed when Hercules struck him with an arrow that had been dipped in the Hydra's venom.

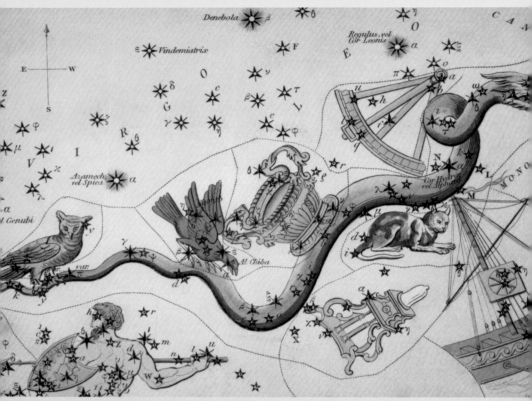

A sky chart from the 1820s depicts an image of the Hydra to illustrate the constellation named after the legendary monster.

As soon as Hercules donned the tunic, the warmth from his body heated the coat and the Hydra venom in the blood. The venom made Hercules' body burn like a thousand fires. He remained too strong to die, but the pain became unbearable as the coat cooked his skin. When he removed the tunic, it tore his flesh, and his suffering continued. Finally Hercules ordered his men to build a funeral **pyre**, and he lay down. He gave his bow and the

Hydra

arrows laced with poison to a friend. As his men lit the fire and flames leaped up around Hercules, a tremendous clap of thunder sounded. Zeus shouted a command, and Hercules rose up into Olympus to join him and the other gods.

According to myth, both Hercules and the Hydra became constellations. Above, the giant serpent stretches across the heavens as the longest constellation. On Earth, fantastic Hydra-like monsters have shown up in stories and writings through the ages.

INCREDIBLE CREATURES

All cultures have stories about creatures that people understand are imaginary. Some legends, however, include things humans have really seen. The Hydra is similar to the make-believe sea monster Scylla, which also appears in Greek tales. She was a violent **kraken-like**, or squid-like, beast that lived on rocks along narrow channels of water. Her six long necks had dog heads. She had sharp teeth, twelve legs, and a fish tail. Scylla grabbed sailors off passing ships and swallowed them alive. Some scholars believe the Hydra and Scylla legends may have come from sightings of the giant octopus or giant squid, whose existence was not proved until 1881. Octopuses have eight arms, which will eventually grow back if cut off. Squid have ten arms. Whalers and sailors throughout the centuries experienced terrifying encounters with the giant ocean creatures. It is possible that the thrashing arms of a giant squid looked like multiple snakes heads attached to one beast. It is also likely that tales about huge ocean animals became exaggerated as they were retold. Real sea creatures may have inspired storytellers to create the incredible Hydra legend.

The Hydra also shows up in Egyptian and Roman myths. In one story from Egypt, people brought offerings to a seven-headed Hydra so he would make the river flow. The Hydra once captured Jinde, a woman who came to the river to get water, and kept her as his wife. Jinde's lover finally cut off the Hydra's heads and freed her. In another tale, a wicked Hydra snake god named Herrut drove the ancient

Egyptian goddess Meh and her husband into the swamps of lower Egypt. Later the Hydra snake god became known as Set, the supreme Egyptian god of evil. The Egyptian Hydra was most often male, while the gender of the Hydra in Roman myths is not clear. The Roman Hydra was a gigantic serpent with 50 snake heads. It tormented doomed souls in Tartarus, a dwelling place for the dead like Hades.

Scylla is another legendary sea monster depicted in Greek mythology with features similar to those of the Hydra. She is said to have attacked sailors at sea by grabbing them off their ships.

To the Egyptians, Romans, and Greeks, the Hydra stood for wickedness and ruin. Some scholars write that the Hydra is similar to the beast mentioned in the book of *Revelation*, the last book of the **Holy Bible**.

BEAST IN THE BIBLE

In *Revelation*, the **prophet** John told of a **vision** in which he saw things that happened in the past and things that would happen in the future. It is believed he recorded the book in the period A.D. 68–96. In the vision, symbols represented beings, objects, and events. A red snake or dragon with seven heads appears in *Revelation* 12:1–10.

> A great and wondrous sign appeared in heaven: a woman clothed with the sun, with the moon under her feet and a crown of twelve stars on her head. She was pregnant and . . . about to give birth. Then another sign appeared in heaven: an enormous red dragon with seven heads and ten horns and seven crowns on his heads. His tail swept a third of the stars out of the sky and flung them to the earth. The dragon stood in front of the woman who was about to give birth, so that he might devour her child the moment it was born. She gave birth to a son, a male child, who will rule all the nations with an iron scepter. And her child was snatched up to God and to his throne. The woman fled into the desert to a place prepared for her by God. . . .
>
> And there was war in heaven. Michael and his angels fought against the dragon, and

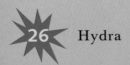 Hydra

A medieval text illustrates the description found in the book of Revelation of a seven-headed dragon, a symbol of evil, accompanied by a pregnant woman with stars on her head and the moon at her feet.

the dragon and his angels fought back. The great dragon was hurled down—that ancient serpent called the devil, or Satan, who leads the whole world astray. He was hurled to the earth, and his angels with him.[2]

In John's vision, the great multi-headed serpent symbolized pure evil or the ultimate wicked power. Although a many-headed beast is written about in the *Bible* and in stories from Egypt and Rome, it is the Greek Hercules tale that made the Hydra a famous monster of destruction. The name *hydra* has long been applied to things that range from terrible to merely troublesome. It is used to refer to a many-sided problem that gets worse each time a solution is tried. The Greeks said about such situations that a person was "cutting off a Hydra." Today people say a crisis is "hydra-headed." Yet the name has also been borrowed to describe things that are useful and good.

CHAPTER 3

THE HYDRA SURVIVES

The name *hydra* covers a wide range of things. An island in Greece is called by the name. A tiny relative of the jellyfish is known as the freshwater hydra. The name has been used as the title of music albums by the bands Toto and Satariel and for the titles of books and a magazine. The snake monster's name and image have inspired the creation of works of art, movies, and toys. Machines and equipment, large and small, bear the name. Scientists have also given the name to other heavenly bodies besides the constellation Hydra.

In 2006 astronomers discovered two new moons of Pluto and named them Nix and Hydra. It is fitting that Hydra serves as a moon to Pluto since Pluto was the Roman god of the underworld.

A small freshwater creature known as the hydra because of its many tentacle-like buds is related to the jellyfish.

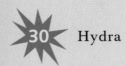 Hydra

In addition, Hydra-Centaurus is the name of a super-cluster, a collection of groups of neighboring stars.

HYDRA COMPUTER SYSTEMS

Far below the heavens, the name *hydra* has been applied to computers and programs. These systems serve many complicated functions or have numerous parts like the monster. Hydra, a computer that plays chess, appeared in 2005. The machine has

British chess grandmaster Michael Adams holds a chess piece against a projection of a powerful computerized chess game called Hydra, which utilizes a network of computers to determine its moves.

multiple computers, each with its own brain, or processor, that searches enormous numbers of positions per second. A human operator works with the Hydra. The person records the plays made by Hydra's opponent and then makes the chess move the Hydra decides on. In its first year, the Hydra won seventeen out of twenty chess matches against humans and other machines. Another namesake is a software project designed to test for weak passwords on computer systems. Developed to show how easily simple and poorly selected passwords could be cracked, it was made for legal use only. The Hydra Game Development Kit is a software program that allows numerous games to be created for it.

SCARY SCREEN STARS

Computers are used to produce or generate Hydra characters for TV and movies. Computer-generated and -animated snake monsters appeared in three TV shows. The beasts are named after the legendary serpent because of their size and multiple heads. In 1994 Starz/Anchor Bay Studios first aired the TV series *Hercules: The Legendary Journeys.* Played by Kevin Sorbo, the hero slays a computer-made Hydra in the episode "Hercules and the Amazon Women." The monster bears three heads, a dragon tail, and a thick brown body with realistic snake markings.

Godzilla: The Series is an animated show by Sony Pictures. In one episode two teenage boys disappear

The Hydra, rendered by special effects, battles Jason (played by Todd Armstrong) in 1963's Jason and the Argonauts, *one of several depictions of the monster in movies and on television.*

into an old mine shaft. They are found wrapped in silver cocoons by their rescuers. Two other characters are attacked by double-headed, liquid-metal monsters called the Silver Hydra. They sling streams of silver to trap humans and even Godzilla himself for a while. Later the two monsters combine into one enormous creature that has thick legs like tree trunks and long pincers on its face.

In the animated Disney series *Hercules*, the Hydra is a huge, black reptile that attacks the hero. In one episode, "The Return of Typhon," the Hydra's father rises to fight again. While all of Olympus celebrates Zeus's victory over Typhon and Echidna, Zeus allows his son Hercules to throw a thunderbolt. The lightning weapon almost destroys Olympus. It accidentally uncovers the mountain that imprisons Typhon and frees him temporarily. He appears as a fiery orange, multi-headed reptile monster.

On the big screen, the Hydra has appeared in many foreign and American films about Hercules. In movies from the 1950s and 1960s, Hercules fights creatures that resemble big toys compared with the computer-generated monsters of today. In the 1960s Vidmark/Trimark movie *Hercules and the Hydra*, the hero battles a three-headed Hydra. Hercules chops off one head, but then he gets knocked out when he bumps into one of the beast's other heads. A 1963 Sony movie, *Jason and the Argonauts*, stars Todd Armstrong and Nancy Kovack. It tells the story of Jason, a Greek hero. He leads a team of adventurers, which includes Hercules, on a dangerous journey to find the Golden Fleece. They battle a seven-headed blue Hydra and skeletons that sword fight. The 2005 Lions Gate movie *Hercules*, with actors Sean Astin and Kim Coates, offers better special effects. The gigantic, gray Hydra has a wide, flat body with a long tail. She has lifelike

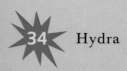

snake heads and necks that move realistically as they circle to attack Hercules.

An animated Hydra carries on the legend in the 1997 Disney movie *Hercules*. The monster has a black dragon body; a long, forked dragon tail; and three snake necks with snake heads. Hercules battles the beast with his sword and a huge slab of stone he rips from the Earth.

Fun and Games

Hydras of different kinds continue to fight battles in computer games, comic books, and toy series. Female warriors known as the Sisters of Battle drive the Hydra flak tank in Warhammer 40,000, the fantasy game by Games Workshop. In a 2006 issue of *Xena, Warrior Princess*, the comic book series by Dynamite Entertainment, Xena and her friend Gabrielle confront a hydra. The beast attacks a ship. Passengers Xena and Gabrielle swiftly kill the fiend. *Hydra* is a comic book series from Marvel Universe that first appeared in 1965 and features an imaginary terrorist organization. The international group Hydra is determined to conquer the world. Hydra's members are mostly men. Lara Brown, however, the daughter of a leader, once had the title Madame Hydra. The group's motto is based on the ability of the Lernaean Hydra to grow new heads. The organization claims it rebuilds and comes back even stronger after a defeat.

The characters in the *Hydra* comic book series also appear as action figures. Other toy sets offer stuffed, plush Hydras and plastic she-monsters in various poses. Some toy series include Hydra, her family, Hercules, and additional characters from TV shows and movies. Most toy Hydras do not have nine heads. They have three to seven heads and are usually blue, red, gray, or green. Hydra and his brother Buster are two characters in the Transformers toy line by Hasbro. In the Transformer universe, they were humans who were bonded with mechanical bodies that transform into jet engines. The Hydra figure does not resemble a many-headed snake in any way, but it does have multiple abilities and weapons.

HYDRA AS FINE ART

Works of art portray the Hydra in ways closer to her original legend. The monster and her fight with Hercules appear on postage stamps. They adorn ancient urns, coins, eating utensils, and plaques carved of ivory. In about the 15th century, an artist crafted a cup of jasper, a fine stoneware, in the shape of a Hydra with seven heads. Through the centuries, artists have reproduced the beast in paintings and sculptures that are found in major cities and museums around the world. The painting *Hercules and the Hydra*, made in about 1475 by Italian artist Antonio del Pollaiuolo, is one example. It shows Hercules in a struggle with an almost black

Antonio del Pollaiuolo's Hercules and the Hydra *(c. 1475) is one of many fine-art depictions of the legendary battle between the hero and the monster.*

A 16th-century jasper cup is adorned with Hercules and the Hydra, both in gold, engaged in battle.

Hydra

Hydra. The American painter John Singer Sargent (1856–1925) completed a painting by the same name. His Hydra is blue and has fifteen snake heads, each with a flaming mouth. One of the most dramatic and beautiful pieces of art based on the Hydra is the larger-than-life-size marble piece *Heracles and the Hydra*. It stands in Helsingør, Denmark. It depicts Hercules in battle against an enormous serpent with more than a dozen heads.

HIGH-TECH HYDRAS

Combat vessels and equipment are named for the battle-ready monster, as are powerful machines that perform multiple tasks. Eight ships of the British Royal Navy have been named Her or His Majesty's Ship (HMS) *Hydra*. The emblem of the ships shows a serpent with seven heads, and the Latin motto is "Like Hercules Persevere." The U.S. military uses a weapon called the Hydra 70 rocket. It carries multiple missiles that are fired from helicopters. One of the most fun things named after the creature is the Hydra Spyder made by Cool Amphibious Manufacturers International. It is a custom car powered by a Corvette engine. Like the beast, the vehicle travels well on land and sea.

Another fun namesake is the rollercoaster Hydra the Revenge. It lies in wait at Dorney Park & Wildwater Kingdom in South Whitehall Township, Pennsylvania. The image of a giant, nine-headed serpent greets visitors to the ride. The huge middle head bares its fangs and sticks out of the sign. The green, looping tracks of the coaster resemble squirming snakes. The Hydra takes riders on a nonstop series of twists, turns, rolls, drops, and spirals. The floorless, steel roller coaster drops passengers 105 feet (32m) while they race over 3,198 feet (975m) of track. When passengers hang upside down, a camera snaps their photographs. The ride speeds into a series of rapid rolls like the corkscrew roll and cobra roll, which make the riders feel weightless. Hydra the Revenge now stands where the old wooden coaster called Hercules once stood. It is said the immortal head of Hydra that Hercules buried has risen there—at last to triumph over Hercules.

The nine-headed serpent of Lake Lerna continues to inspire new make-believe monsters and multiple namesakes. The Hydra legend, like her eternal head, seems to live forever.

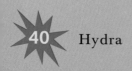

Hydra

NOTES

CHAPTER 1: GREAT MULTI-HEADED MONSTER

1. Pausanias, translated by W. H. S. Jones, *Description of Greece, I: Books 1-2 (Attica and Corinth)*. Massachusetts: Loeb Classical Library, 1969, 2.37.5,6. http://209.85.141.104/search?q=cache:Fy3f7sYvkJ0J:www.theoi.com/Text/Pausanias2C.html+Pausanias+Nero+Alcyonian+Lake&hl=en&ct=clnk&cd=5&gl=us.

CHAPTER 2: HYDRA REARS HER UGLY HEADS

2. *Revelation* 12:1–10. New International Version. Grand Rapids, MI: Zondervan, 1979.

GLOSSARY

centaur: One of a race of monsters having the head, trunk, and arms of a man, and the body and legs of a horse.

geologists: Scientists who study the origin, history, and structure of the earth.

Hades: Dwelling place of the dead in Greek mythology.

Holy Bible: The collection of sacred writings of the Christian religion, made up of the Old Testament and New Testament.

kraken-like: That which resembles the multi-tentacled kraken, a sea monster proven to be a giant squid in 1881.

oracle of Delphi: A priestess who gave advice in the most important Greek shrine, dating back to 1400 B.C.

prophet: A person who speaks for God or by divine inspiration.

pyre: A pile of burning wood on which a dead body may be cremated.

venom: The poisonous fluid that some animals

42

like snakes and spiders produce and put into their victims by biting, stinging, and so on.

vision: An experience in which things appear clearly to the mind, although not actually present, by divine or other means.

FOR FURTHER EXPLORATION

BOOKS

Ingri D'Aulaire and Edgar Parin, *Book of Greek Myths*. Garden City, NY: Doubleday, 1980. This book is full of interesting sketches and entertaining stories that provide a detailed account of Greek mythology.

Doris Gates, *Mightiest of Mortals, Heracles*. New York: Viking, 1975. This book retells the exploits and twelve labors of the Greek hero Hercules, or Heracles, in a well-written, storybook format.

Kerry Usher, *Heroes, Gods and Emperors from Roman Mythology*. New York: Schocken, 1984. This fun read on Roman myths and life in ancient Rome has beautiful, full-page color pictures.

INTERNET SOURCES

Ron Leadbetter, "Hydra," *Encyclopedia Mythica*. www.pantheon.org/articles/h/hydra.html. This site recounts the legend of the Hydra.

Theoi Project, "Hydra." www.theoi.com/Ther/DrakonHydra.html. This section of the Theoi Project Web site provides extensive information on Greek mythology and its influence on classical literature and art. It has a gallery of colorful pictures and a guide to the gods, spirits, fabulous creatures, and heroes of ancient Greek mythology.

ThinkQuest, "Hercules' Adventures: The Lernaean Hydra." http://library.thinkquest.org/26264/myths/tales/heroes/site2002.htm. There is a wonderful picture of the Hydra and fun information about Hercules and his adventures on these Web pages.

WEB SITES

The Constellation Hydra, LMS Planetarium (www.coldwater.k12.mi.us/lms/planetarium/myth/hydra.html). An outline of the Hydra constellation on this site shows how people might see it as a snake shape. There is also information about the myths connected to the Hydra constellation and other nearby constellations.

The Creatures Library, HowStuffWorks (http://reference.howstuffworks.com/greek-roman-creatures-encyclopedia-channel.htm). This site provides information on creatures from Greek and Roman mythology and also on the ancient cultures of Greece and Rome.

Lernaean Hydra, Hellenica (www.mlahanas.de/Greeks/Mythology/LernaeanHydra.html). This Web site features many pieces of art and objects based on the Hydra. The items range from ancient coins, paintings, and urns to huge marble statues and even the Hydra 70 rocket.

INDEX

Picture Credits

Cover illustration: William Canavan

The Art Archive/Bibliotheque Municipale Valenciennes/Gianni Dagli Orti, 27

Columbia/The Kobal Collection, 33

Echidna, from the 'Parco dei Mostri' (Monster Park) by Pirro Ligorio (c. 1500–83) 1552 (photo),/Sacro Bosco di Bomarzo, Lazio, Italy/The Bridgeman Art Library, 9

Hercules and the Lernaean Hydra, after Gustave Moreau, c. 1876 (oil on canvas) (detail of 226576), Berchere, Narcisse (1819–91)/Musee Gustave Moreau, Paris, France, Lauros/Giraudon/The Bridgeman Art Library, 5

Hulton Archive/Getty Images, 17, 20

Erich Lessing/Art Resource, NY, 12, 25, 37

Library of Congress/Science Faction/Getty Images, 22

Mansell/Time Life Pictures/Getty Images, 7

John D. McHugh/AFP/Getty Images, 31

Scala/Art Resource, NY, 38

Scala/Ministero per i Beni e le Attivita culturali/Art Resource, NY, 14-15

Spike Walker/Stone/Getty Images, 30

About the Author

Jennifer Guess McKerley enjoys writing fiction and nonfiction for all ages. Her other nonfiction books for children include *Man o' War, Best Racehorse Ever, Amazing Armadillos, Goblins,* and *The Kraken.* Her book of fiction is *There Goes Turtle's Hat.* She enjoys living in New Mexico. You can visit her Web site at www.jenniferguessmckerley.com.